THE DALLAS COWBOYS

Sloan MacRae

PowerKiDS press.

New York

Published in 2010 by The Rosen Publishing Group, Inc.
29 East 21st Street, New York, NY 10010

First Edition

Editor: Amelie von Zumbusch
Book Design: Greg Tucker
Photo Researcher: Jessica Gerweck

Photo Credits: Cover (Roger Staubach), p. 17 Focus on Sport/Getty Images; cover (background), pp. 5, 7 Ronald Martinez/Getty Images; cover (Troy Aikman), p. 9 George Rose/Getty Images; cover (Emmitt Smith), pp. 19, 22 (bottom) Elsa Hasch/AllSport/Getty Images; p. 11 Scott Boehm/Getty Images; pp. 13, 22 (top) Robert Riger/Getty Images; p. 15 Tony Tomsic/Getty Images; p. 21 Jim McIsaac/Getty Images.

Library of Congress Cataloging-in-Publication Data

MacRae, Sloan.
  The Dallas Cowboys / Sloan MacRae. — 1st ed.
      p. cm. — (America's greatest teams)
  Includes index.
  ISBN 978-1-4042-8145-5 (library binding) — ISBN 978-1-4358-3394-4 (pbk.) —
ISBN 978-1-4358-3395-1 (6-pack)
  1. Dallas Cowboys (Football team—Juvenile literature. I. Title.
  GV956.D3M33 2010
  796.332'6407642812—dc22
                                    2009007215

CONTENTS

AMERICA'S TEAM

The Dallas Cowboys are from Texas, but they have fans around the world. They are one of the most **popular** teams in the National Football League, or NFL. The Cowboys are known for their flashy, **glamorous** players. These players are fun to watch. The Cowboys are so popular that they are often called America's Team.

The Cowboys are one of the most successful football **franchises**. They have played in more Super Bowls than any other NFL team. Dallas has broken many other records, too. The Cowboys have appeared in the most **postseason** games. They also have the most **consecutive** winning seasons.

Over the years, the Cowboys have had many stars. Today's Cowboys stars include Andre Gurode (left), Tony Romo (middle), and Leonard Davis (right).

RING OF HONOR

You can recognize the Cowboys by the blue stars on their silver **helmets**. The Cowboys' uniforms are blue and white. The Cowboys most often wear white jerseys, or shirts, with blue numbers. They also sometimes wear blue jerseys with white numbers.

Texas Stadium was the home of the Cowboys for 37 years. The stadium was known for the giant ring that circled the field there. It was called the Ring of Honor, and it listed the greatest Cowboys players in team history. In 2009, the Cowboys moved to a brand-new stadium in Arlington, Texas. The new stadium also has a Ring of Honor.

8 TROY AIKMAN 1989-2000

22 EMMITT SMITH 1990-2002

Troy Aikman and Emmitt Smith were among the players listed on the Ring of Honor at the Cowboys' old home, Texas Stadium.

HAPPY THANKSGIVING

The Cowboys listed in the Ring of Honor are among the greatest football players of all time. Many of these players are household names. **Quarterbacks** Roger Staubach and Troy Aikman made Super Bowl history. **Running backs** Tony Dorsett and Emmitt Smith were fast and **agile**. **Wide receiver** Michael Irvin made some of the greatest catches NFL fans have ever seen.

Millions of football fans watch the Cowboys play on national television every Thanksgiving Day. Watching the Cowboys on Thanksgiving is something many American families look forward to every year.

Troy Aikman joined the Cowboys in 1989. He went on to become one of the most successful quarterbacks of the 1990s.

ROWDY AND THE CHEERLEADERS

The Cowboys are popular for other things besides their football players. For example, the team is known for its cheerleaders. The Dallas Cowboys Cheerleaders have their own television show. There are even movies about them. They are probably the best-known cheerleaders in the world. The Cowboys also have a **mascot** named Rowdy. Rowdy looks like a cowboy. He visits schools and makes fans laugh during games.

The Cowboys are more than just a successful team. They are a successful business, too. In fact, many people say that the Cowboys are worth more money than any other American sports franchise. A businessman named Jerry Jones owns the team.

Rowdy became the Cowboys' mascot in 1996. He does many things, such as throw T-shirts to the crowd and make fun of other teams, during games.

11

A TEAM FOR A SONG

Dallas almost missed out on having an NFL team! In the 1950s, NFL leaders were adding new teams. They talked about having one in Dallas. However, the owner of the Washington Redskins knew that a team from Texas would be popular. He argued against having a Dallas team because he wanted everyone living in the South to be a Redskins fan.

Then, the people who wanted to form the Cowboys bought the rights to Washington's fight song. This meant that the Redskins would not be allowed to play their own fight song during games! The Redskins' owner backed down, and the Cowboys took the field in 1960. Dallas and Washington became big **rivals**.

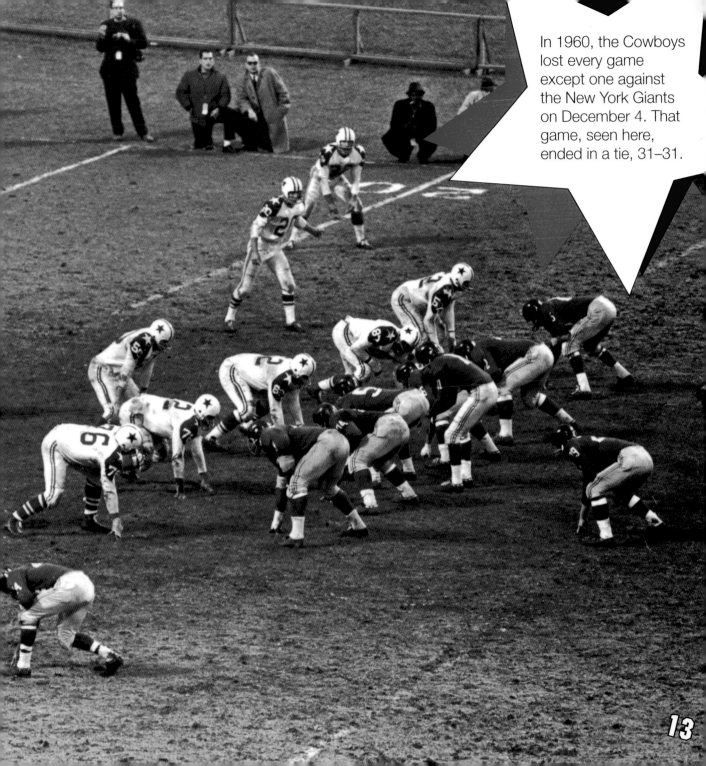

In 1960, the Cowboys lost every game except one against the New York Giants on December 4. That game, seen here, ended in a tie, 31–31.

TOM LANDRY

Tom Landry became the Cowboys' coach in 1960 and stayed with the team for 29 years. He was known for always wearing a kind of hat called a fedora. Landry and the Cowboys struggled for the first few years. Dallas was one of the worst teams in football for much of the 1960s. However, Landry turned the team around and led the Cowboys to 20 consecutive winning seasons. No other coach or team has ever done this.

Landry worked hard to build up the team's **defense**. The team's defense was so successful that the Cowboys' defensive players became known as the Doomsday Defense.

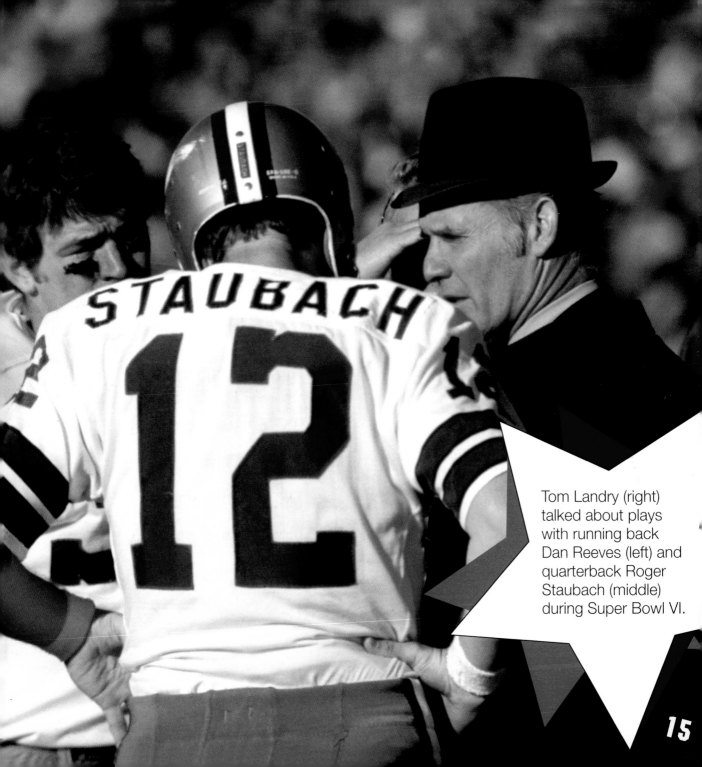

Tom Landry (right) talked about plays with running back Dan Reeves (left) and quarterback Roger Staubach (middle) during Super Bowl VI.

15

BEYOND THE BLUNDER BOWL

The Cowboys became one of the NFL's best teams in the 1970s. Landry coached Dallas to the team's first Super Bowl in 1971. Sadly, the Cowboys played poorly and lost to the Baltimore Colts. Both teams made so many mistakes that people called this game the Blunder Bowl. The next season, the Cowboys played well enough to make it to their second consecutive Super Bowl. Dallas played better this time and beat the Miami Dolphins.

The Cowboys played in five Super Bowls in the 1970s. They won a second NFL **championship** after beating the Denver Broncos. However, Dallas lost two close Super Bowl games to their new rivals, the Pittsburgh Steelers.

The Cowboys won the Super Bowl for the second time in 1978. Butch Johnson (second from right) made a touchdown that helped win that game.

17

THE TRIPLETS

The Cowboys were not as successful during the 1980s. However, they climbed to the top again in the 1990s. They beat the Buffalo Bills in back-to-back Super Bowls. They even beat the Steelers in a Super Bowl in 1996. The Cowboys' win against Pittsburgh was extra sweet because it was their third Super Bowl win within four years. No team had ever done this before!

At this time, the team was led by three players, known as the Triplets. They were quarterback Troy Aikman, wide receiver Michael Irvin, and running back Emmitt Smith. In time, Smith became the NFL's all-time leading rusher. This means he ran for more yards than any player in NFL history.

Emmitt Smith, seen here, played for the Cowboys from 1990 to 2002. In 1993, he was named the NFL's most valuable player, or MVP.

CONTINUING GREATNESS

Today, the Cowboys are once again led by flashy players, such as quarterback Tony Romo and **tight end** Jason Witten. They are still one of the most popular teams in the United States. A study in 2008 found that the Cowboys had more fans than any other NFL team.

The Cowboys look like they will be strong and successful for many years to come. They have a new stadium and young stars. They will likely add more names to the Ring of Honor. Dallas is on track to win more Super Bowl titles and break new records. The Cowboys will play many more Thanksgiving Day games. They will continue to be America's Team.

Tony Romo became the Cowboys' starting quarterback during the 2006 season. He has grown to be one of the NFL's top quarterbacks.

DALLAS COWBOYS TIMELINE

1960
The Dallas Cowboys join the NFL.

1966
The Cowboys have their first winning season.

1972
The Cowboys win their first Super Bowl by beating the Miami Dolphins.

1978
The Cowboys beat the Denver Broncos in Super Bowl XII.

1989
Jimmy Johnson becomes head coach of the Cowboys.

1990
The Cowboys draft, or pick, Emmitt Smith to play on the team.

1994
The Cowboys beat the Buffalo Bills in the Super Bowl for the second time in a row.

2008
The Cowboys play their final game at Texas Stadium.

2002
Emmitt Smith becomes the NFL's all-time leading rusher.

1996
The Cowboys win their third Super Bowl in four years, finally beating the Pittsburgh Steelers.

GLOSSARY

AGILE (A-jul) Able to move easily and gracefully.

CHAMPIONSHIP (CHAM-pee-un-ship) A contest held to decide the best, or the winner.

CONSECUTIVE (ken-SEH-kyuh-tiv) In a row, or back to back.

DEFENSE (DEE-fents) The part of a team that tries to stop another team from scoring.

FRANCHISES (FRAN-chy-zez) Professional sports teams.

GLAMOROUS (GLAM-rus) Interesting and exciting.

HELMETS (HEL-mits) Coverings worn to keep the head safe.

MASCOT (MAS-kot) A person, animal, or object that stands for something.

POPULAR (PAH-pyuh-lur) Liked by lots of people.

POSTSEASON (pohst-SEE-zun) Games played after the regular season.

QUARTERBACKS (KWAHR-ter-baks) Football players who direct a team's plays.

RIVALS (RY-vulz) People or teams who try to get or do the same thing as one another.

RUNNING BACKS (RUN-ing BAKS) Football players who run with the ball, block players from the other team, and sometimes catch the ball.

TIGHT END (TYT END) A football player who mostly blocks other players but sometimes catches the ball.

WIDE RECEIVER (WYD rih-SEE-vur) A football player who runs down the field and catches the ball.

INDEX

WEB SITES

Due to the changing nature of Internet links, PowerKids Press has developed an online list of Web sites related to the subject of this book. This site is updated regularly. Please use this link to access the list:
www.powerkidslinks.com/teams/cowboy/